BLUEPRINTS
History
Key Stage 1
Copymasters

Second Edition

Wendy Clemson

Stanley Thornes (Publishers) Ltd

Do you receive *BLUEPRINTS NEWS*?

Blueprints is an expanding series of practical teacher's ideas books and photocopiable resources for use in primary schools. Books are available for separate infant and junior age ranges for every core and foundation subject, as well as for an ever widening range of other primary teaching needs. These include **Blueprints Primary English** books and **Blueprints Resource Banks**. **Blueprints** are carefully structured around the demands of National Curriculum in England and Wales, but are used successfully by schools and teachers in Scotland, Northern Ireland and elsewhere.

Blueprints provide:
- Total curriculum coverage
- Hundreds of practical ideas
- Books specifically for the age range you teach
- Flexible resources for the whole school or for individual teachers
- Excellent photocopiable sheets – ideal for assessment and children's work profiles
- Supreme value

Books may be bought by credit card over the telephone and information obtained on **(0242) 577944**. Alternatively, photocopy and return this **FREEPOST** form to receive **Blueprints News**, our regular update on all new and existing titles. You may also like to add the name of a friend who would be interested in being on the mailing list.

Please add my name to the **BLUEPRINTS NEWS** mailing list.

Mr/Mrs/Miss/Ms _____

Home address _____

_____ Postcode _____

School address _____

_____ Postcode _____

Please also send **BLUEPRINTS NEWS** to:

Mr/Mrs/Miss/Ms _____

Address _____

_____ Postcode _____

To: Marketing Services Dept., Stanley Thornes Ltd, FREEPOST (GR 782), Cheltenham, GL50 1BR

First published in 1992 by:
Stanley Thornes (Publishers) Ltd
Ellenborough House
Wellington Street
CHELTENHAM GL50 1YD
England

Reprinted 1992
Reprinted 1993
2nd edition 1995

A catalogue record for this book is available from the British Library.

ISBN 0–7487–2219–X

Typeset by Tech-Set, Gateshead, Tyne & Wear.
Printed and bound in Great Britain.

CONTENTS

INTRODUCTION

In this book there are 96 photocopiable copymasters linked to many of the activities in the Teacher's Resource Book. Where the copymasters are referred to in the text of the Teacher's Resource Book there are instructions on how to use them. They are referred to by number in the Teacher's Resource Book by this symbol . The copymasters reinforce and extend activities in the Teacher's Resource Book and provide opportunities to record activities and results in an organised way. When the children have completed these copymasters they can be added to work files or used as exemplar material in pupil profiles. You may also wish to use completed copymasters as a resource for your assessments. There are two record sheets at the back of this book, one for the children's own self-appraisal and one for you to make your comments on their National Curriculum experience.

The copymasters are organised into fifteen key infants topics which are covered in depth in the Teacher's Resource Book. Sheets 79–96 develop general historical skills for Key Stage 1. You will find explanation of how to use them at the front of the Teacher's Resource Book.

Name: _____

Family tree

◯ :draw face   ▭ :write name

My grandparents

My parents

Me

Happy families

Name: _____

Happy families

Name: _____

Then and now

Do you think families often had/have these things **in Victorian times** or **now**?

The first one is done for you.

~~Victorian~~ Now~~	Victorian Now	Victorian Now
washing machine	quill pens	oil lamps
Victorian Now	Victorian Now	Victorian Now
car	trainers	radio
Victorian Now	Victorian Now	Victorian Now
dinners	candles	family Bible
Victorian Now	Victorian Now	Victorian Now
TV	top hats	holidays abroad
Victorian Now	Victorian Now	Victorian Now
open fire	electric iron	copper kettle

Name: _____

Family likeness

My looks

join where alike

My _____ 's looks

draw

My personality

My _____ 's personality

write

Words for looks: chin, nose, fat, hair, thin, straight, tall, curly, short, colour, hands, eyes, mouth, eyebrows

Words for personality: loving, quiet, temper, strong, shy, skill, friendly, kind, happy, generous, sad, lively

Name: _____

Homes timeline

Colour. Cut out. Put in order.

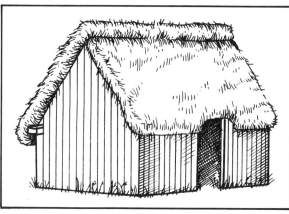

Name: _____

Doors

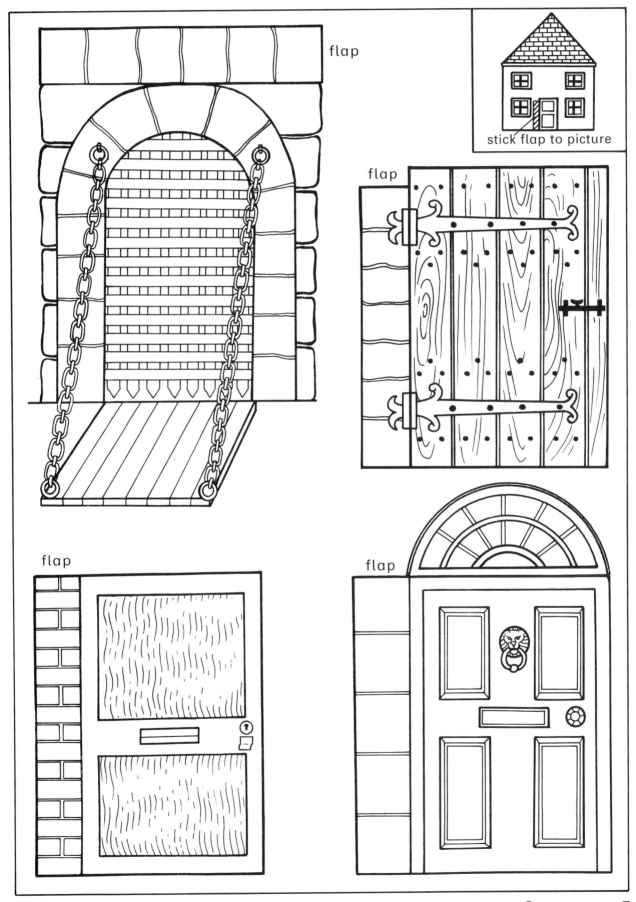

flap

stick flap to picture

flap

flap

flap

Name: _____

Living space

My living room
(draw or write)

Name: _____

Doing the washing

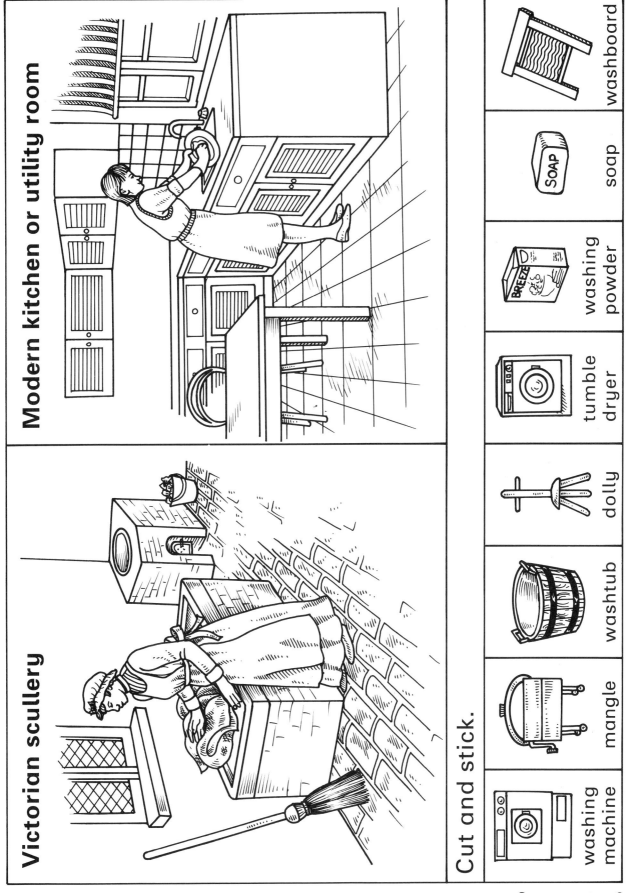

Victorian scullery

Modern kitchen or utility room

Cut and stick.

washing machine	mangle	washtub	dolly	tumble dryer	washing powder	soap	washboard

Museum story

Write the story.

Name: _____

My garden

How my garden looks.

Things that grow in my garden.

What my garden is for.

Picture writing

My code

Picture					
Meaning	I/me				

Picture					
Meaning					

My code message

Name: _____

Seals

My seal (draw)

How I made my seal.

What a seal is for.

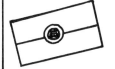 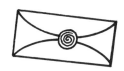 

Name: _____

Message timeline

Cut out. Put in order.

Telling.

Send it by letter post.

Put it on the mail coach.

Send it with a messenger on horseback.

Fax it.

Name: _____

Keeping a diary

My diary for _____ **in** _____
Mondays, Tuesdays, Wednesdays,   (month)
Thursdays, Fridays

Date _____

Date _____

Date _____

Date _____

Date _____

Name: _____

Illuminated initials

Add your initial to each pattern.
Finish and colour the patterns.

Make your own initial patterns here.

Name: _____

Wearing clothes

Why I wear clothes
(draw)

| my warm clothes | clothes that keep me cool |
| clothes that keep me safe | clothes that show I belong to a group |

Name: _____

Fabric sort

Sort the fabrics into sets.

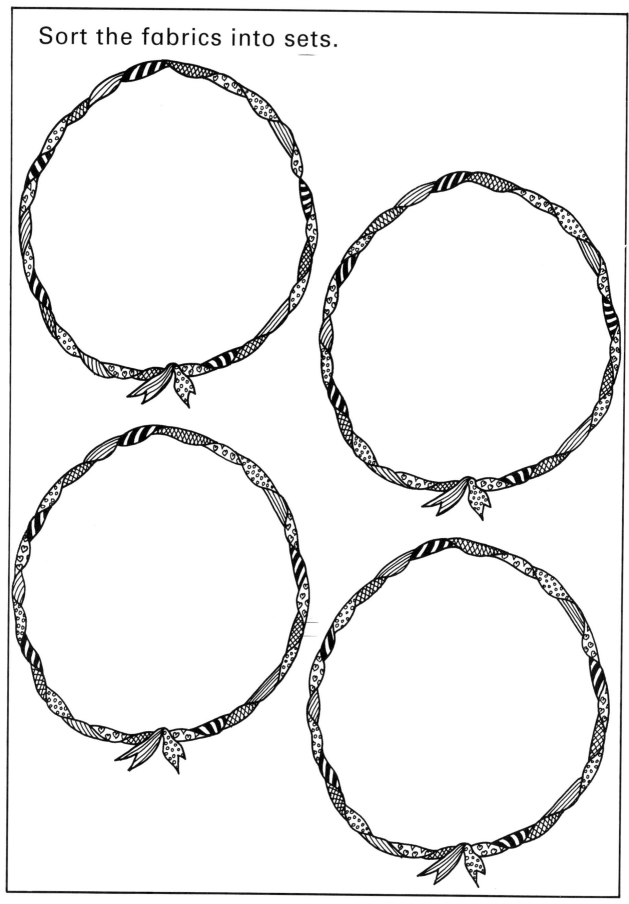

Name: _____

Work clothes

Which toys belong here?

Ring the toys that do not belong because they had not been invented.

A shoebox theatre

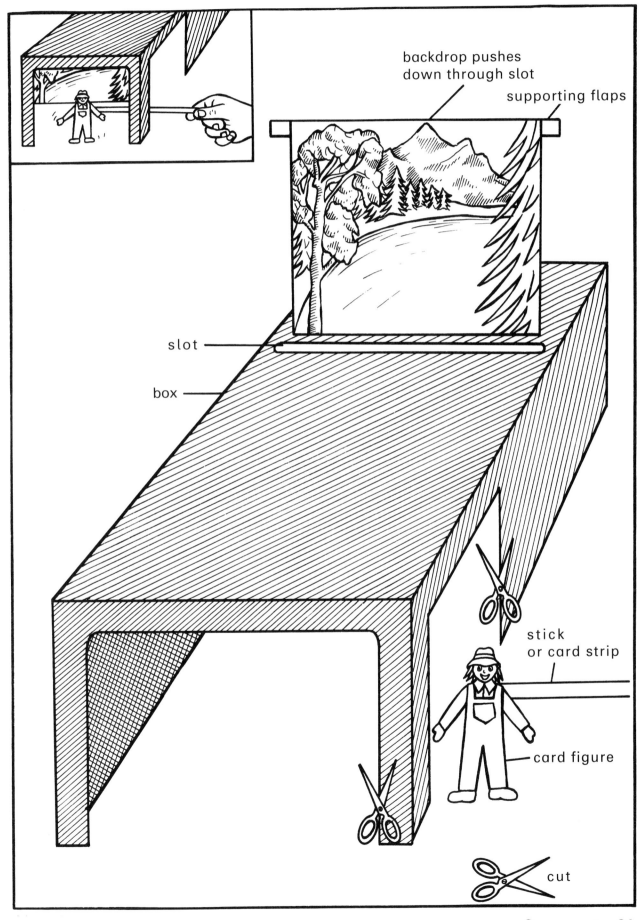

backdrop pushes
down through slot

supporting flaps

slot

box

stick
or card strip

card figure

cut

Name: _____

A paper puppet ▷

Stick on to card. Cut out.
Fix together with 4 paper-fasteners.

a paper-fastener

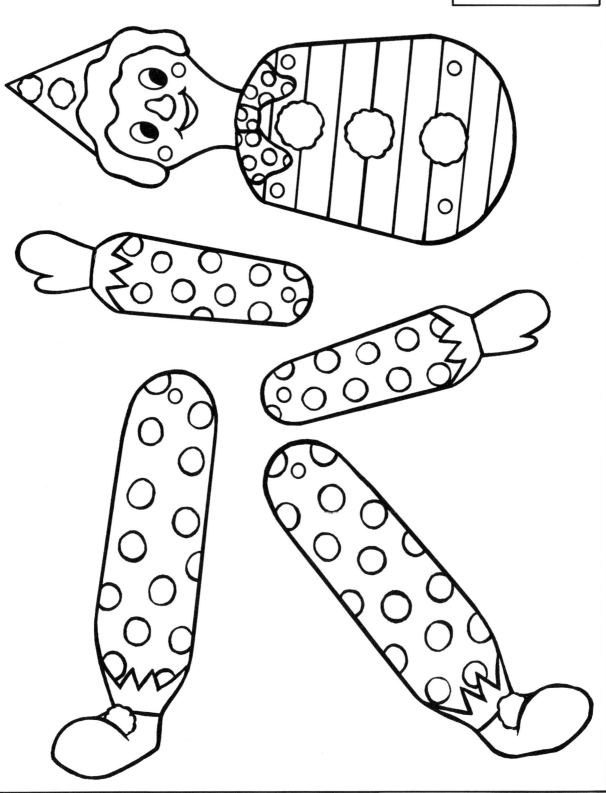

Name: _____

Rhymes

clap

clap clap

stamp stamp stamp

one

two

three

la la

heel and toe

sing sing

jump dance

clap tap tap

tap

Copymaster 23

Name: _____

Games long ago

Name: _____

My seaside souvenir

Draw.

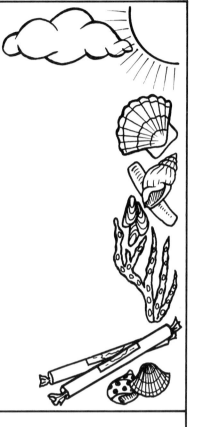

What is it? _____

How old is it? _____

Where does it come from? _____

Tell its story.

Draw your own postcard

Come to sunny ....

Postcard designed by ....

Name: _____

Postcard timeline

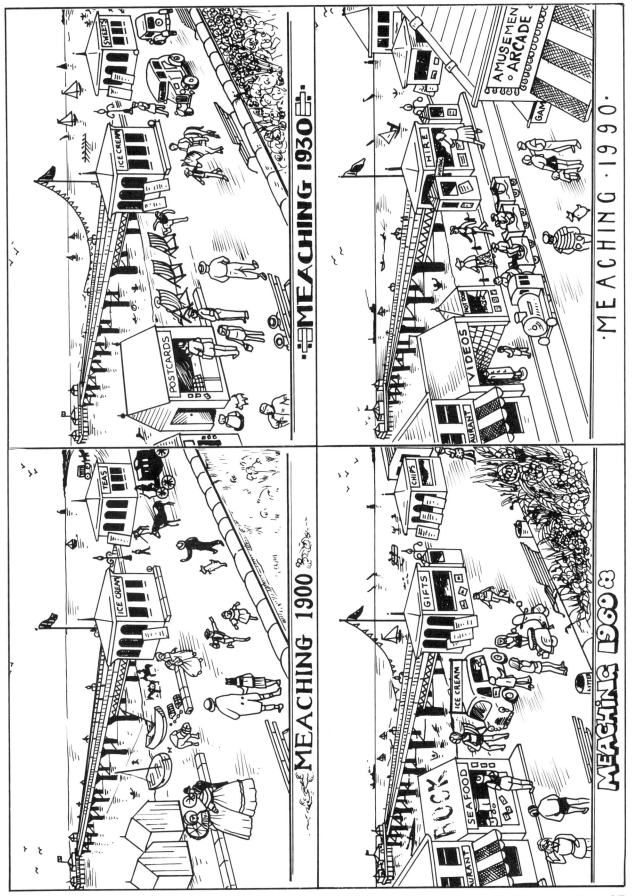

Swimwear

1960

1925

1990

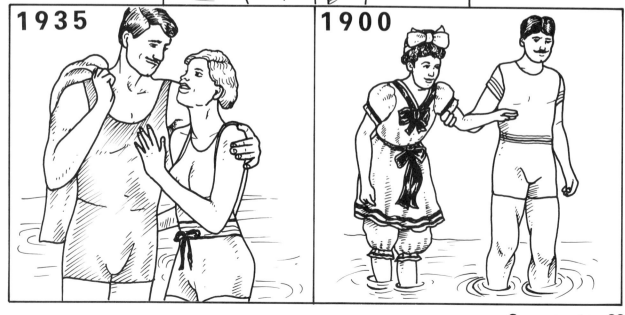

1935

1900

Name: _____

A seaside resort

1800

1860

1930

1990

My teacher

What my teacher says.	Things my teacher does in class.	My teacher looks like this.

All about my school

Name of school	
Head teacher	
Number of teachers	
Teachers' names	
Number of children in my class	
Number of children in school	
Number of classrooms	
Number of buildings	
Other	

Name: _____

Grown-ups' schooldays

Did boys and girls do the same work?

What good things happened in school?

What were school dinners like?

What happened when you were naughty?

What did your school look like?

What did you do at school?

What happened when you did good work?

What was school like?

When did school start?

Was there a playground?

A story-book school

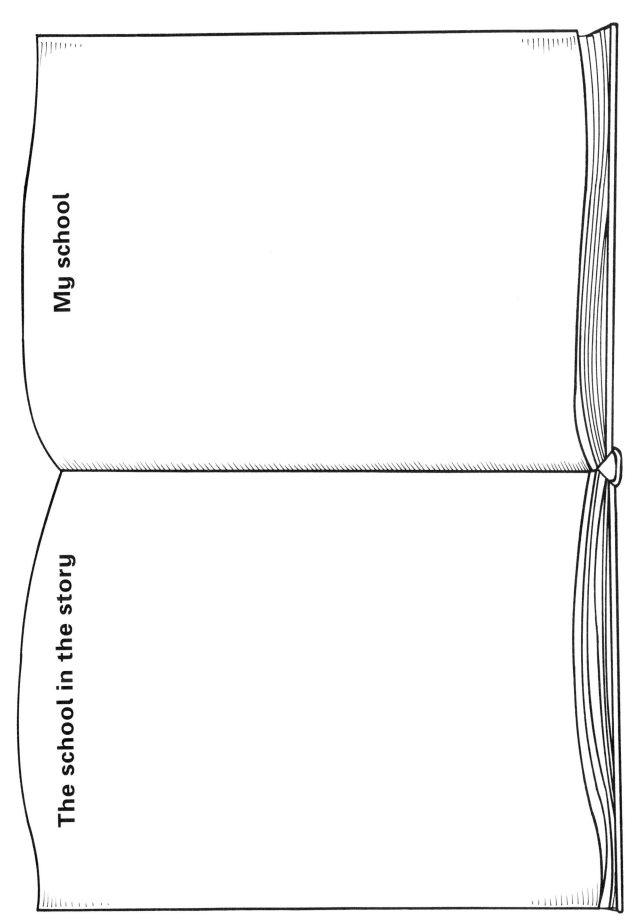

My school

The school in the story

Name: _____

Schoolrooms long ago and now

Clothes for school

Edwardian schoolchildren

Schoolchildren today

Name: _____

Being a child

Mum's or Dad's childhood

I talked to my _____.

I asked about these things.

Favourite clothes

Friends

Games

Evenings

Pocket-money

TV

Other things

Name: _____

My Mum/Dad and me

My Mum's or Dad's childhood	Me as a child now

Name: _____

Looking back

In our great-grandparents' time

In our grandparents' time

In our parents' time

Name: _____

My picture-story

Draw pictures to tell a story.

What is the warning in this story?

All about food

My favourite foods

Food-tasting record

Name of food	Looks	Taste	Texture	Star rating

Name: _____

Cooking in the past ▷

Cut out the pictures. Put them in order.

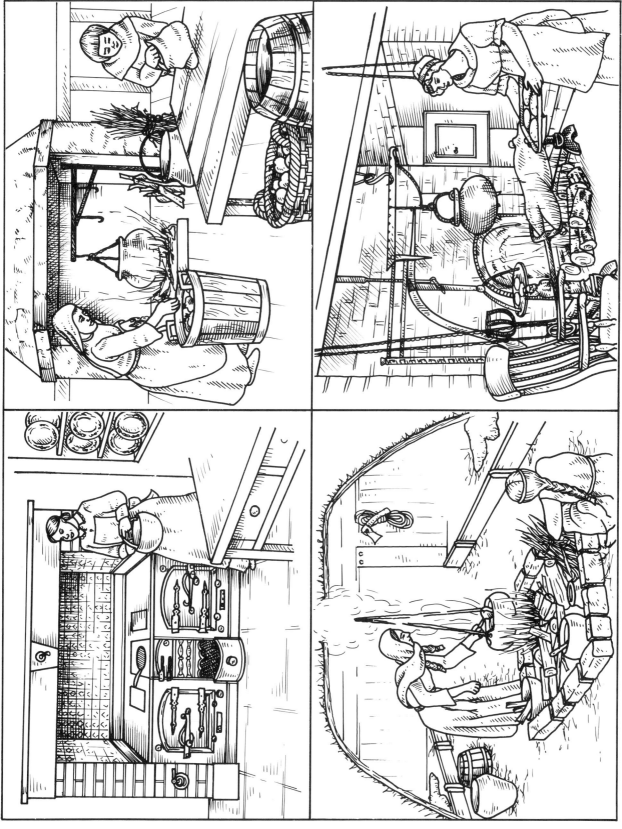

Name: _____

Cutlery

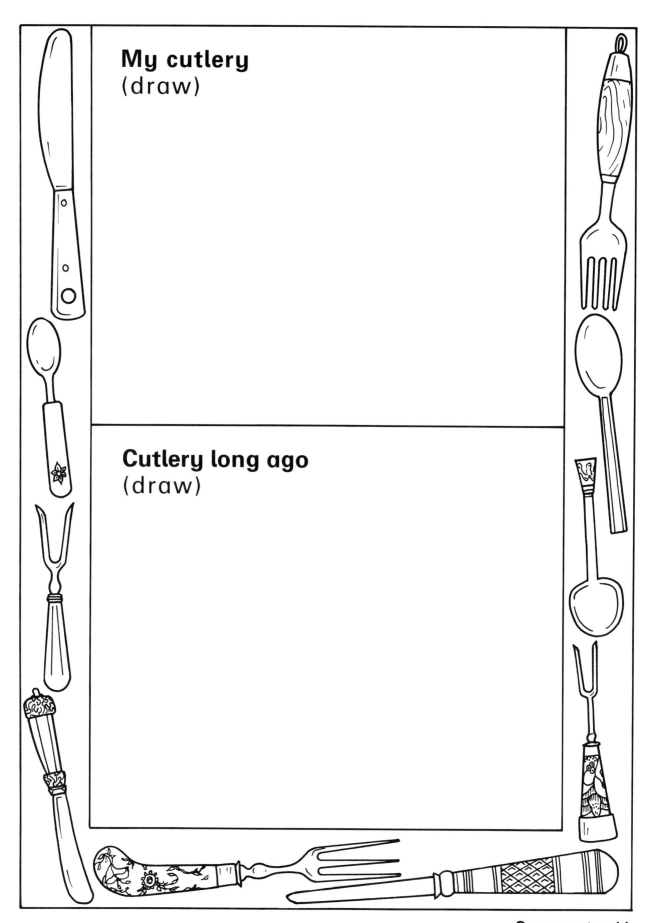

My cutlery
(draw)

Cutlery long ago
(draw)

Name: _____

Meals through the ages

Roman times
2000 years ago

Medieval times
700 years ago

Tudor times
400 years ago

Victorian times
100 years ago

Now
The 1990s

Name: _____

The family car

Our car
(draw)

Make and model _____

More about our car

Name: _____

Family memories of transport

Their memories	People I talked to

What to ask

Have you ever been on a steam train? A trolleybus? A tram?
Tell me about the traffic when you were young.
How did you travel long ago? Where did you go?

Name: _____

Road transport in history

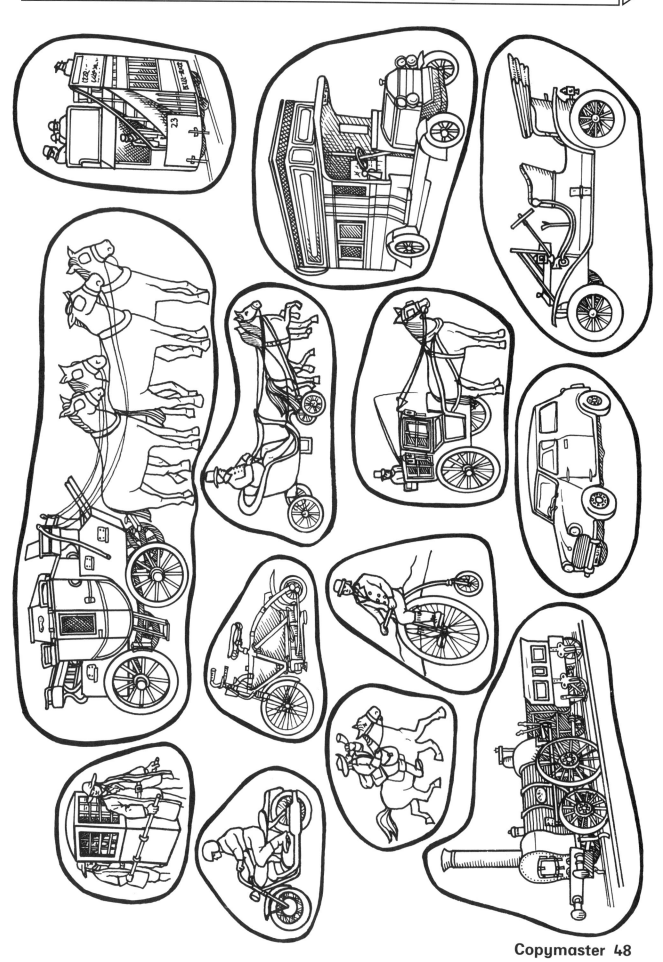

Name: _____

Signposts

A signpost (draw and write)

On my signpost, the nearest place is _____

It is _____ miles away.

How long would it take to get there

on foot? _____

on horseback? _____

by bike? _____

by car? _____

Name: _____

Boats and ships

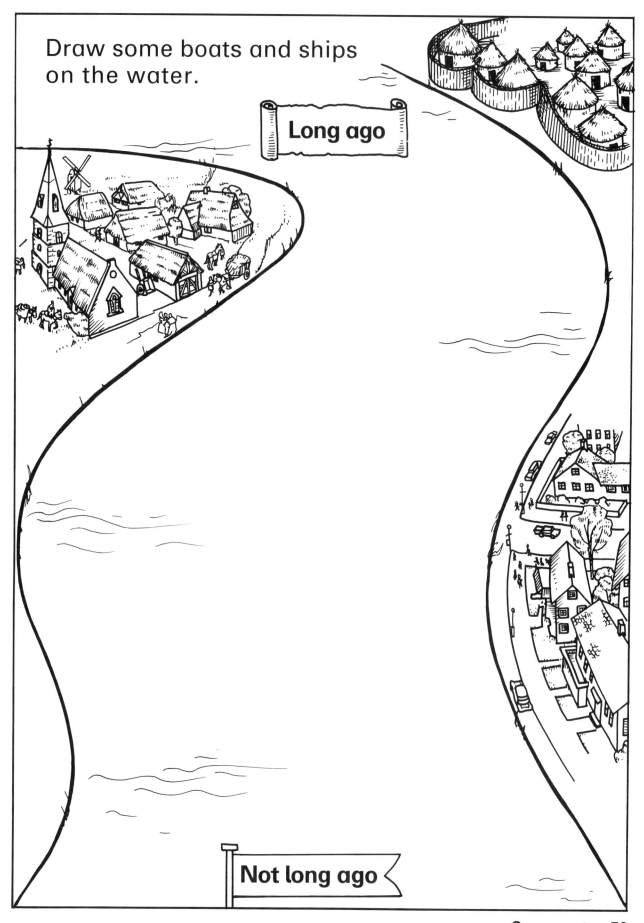

Draw some boats and ships on the water.

Long ago

Not long ago

Name: _____

Information about jobs

Job	Name of person

Changes in farming

Draw or write about 3 changes in farming.

1

2

3

Name: _____

Craftwork

This is the craft called _____.

A person who does it is called a _____.

This is how it is done. (draw or write)

How did this person learn the craft?

What tools are used?

Are there still people doing this craft?

Name: _____

A look at some crafts

A cobbler

A thatcher

A blacksmith

A potter

A cabinet-maker

A basketmaker

Name: _____

Working as a servant

Why I should not like to be a servant.

Don't run.

Come here.

Do this!
Do that!

You are late again.

Be silent!

Answer that bell.

This is not good enough.

Name: _____

Inside a Victorian house

Pets

A pet called _____
(draw)

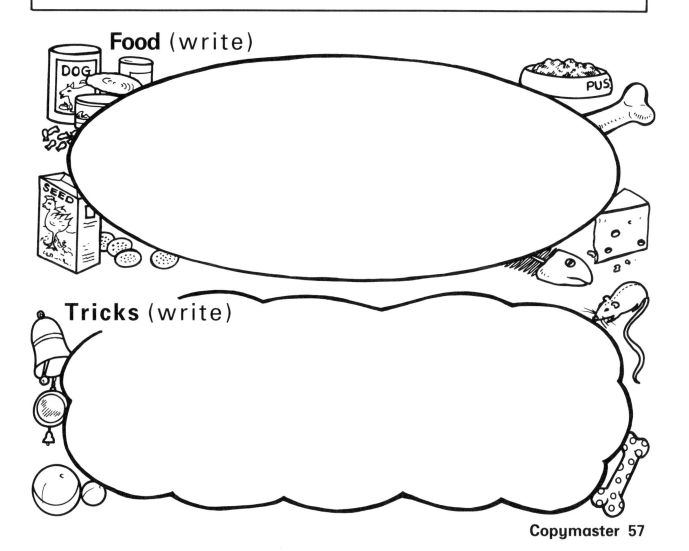

Food (write)

Tricks (write)

Name: _____

Dogs

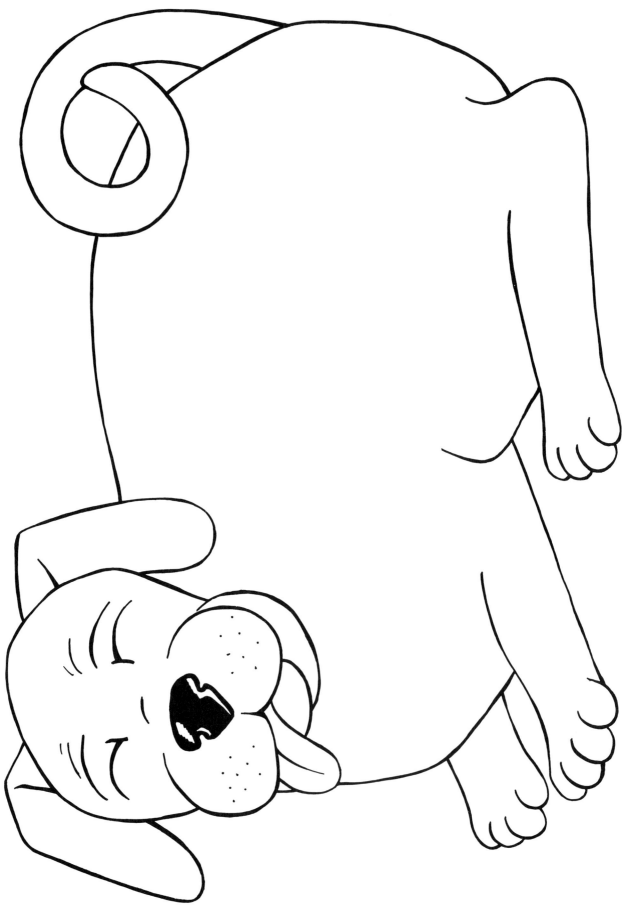

Name: _____

Cats

Pet stories

A pet story I like ...

Facts about pets in the past ...

Name: _____

Horses then and now

Animal badges, logos and emblems

Animal designs

Thinking about shopping

The story of the _____ I buy.

Name: _____

Barter

Name: _____

Shopping in the past

Who I talked to _____

When you were young where did your Mum
go shopping?

_____

_____

What sorts of shops were there? _____

_____

_____

Tell me about a shop that is not the same
as it was when you were young.

_____

_____

_____

_____

A medieval market

Name: _____

A day at the market

Draw things on sale.

Draw the stallholder.

Draw what the stallholder wants to take home.

Families and their needs

The Cost of Living in 1950

Essential weekly spending
Food £2   Heat and Light £1   Clothing 50p
Shelter £1·25 rent **OR** £2·75 mortgage

Other essential costs
Weekly pocket money; Mike's bus fares; John's travel to work.

Prices of other items

Travel
Bicycle £12
Car £575
Petrol 15p (gallon)
Road tax £12
Bus fares $\frac{1}{2}$ p
per mile

Household goods
Cooker £16   Bed £30
Fridge £50   Table £20
Vacuum   Chair £10
cleaner £30   Lounge
Fire £10   suite £50
Washing   Bedroom
machine £30   suite £90

Entertainment and Leisure
Newspapers 5p a week
Comics 7p a week
Cinema 10p (adult)
        5p (child)
Bag of sweets about 2p
Tube of fruit gums 1p

Radio £25 (plus £1
    licence per year)
TV £75 (plus £3
    licence per year
Record player £14
A family seaside holiday
    in Britain for 1 week
    approximately £20

The Cotton Family in 1950

John Cotton, aged 35, is a skilled tool-maker. He works 7 miles away in the nearest town and earns £7 a week.

Winnifred Cotton, aged 32, has a part-time job locally. She earns £2.50 a week.

Lucy Cotton, aged 12. She walks to school. Lucy gets 10p a week pocket-money.

Mike Cotton, aged 10. He catches the bus to and from school, which is 4 miles away. Mike also gets 10p a week pocket-money.

The family's essential needs are:
Food   Heat and Light   Clothing
Shelter (they must pay rent or a mortgage)

Other needs (not essential) are:
Entertainment and Leisure
Holidays
Home improvement

Copymaster 68

From grocery store to supermarket

Name: _____

Harvest Festival

All about
Harvest Festival

Name: _____

Christmas now

Name: _____

A Victorian Christmas

Name: _____

Choose your own celebration

A special day

Roman numerals

I	II	III	IV	V	VI	VII	VIII	IX	X
1	2	3	4	5	6	7	8	9	10

L	C	D	M
50	100	500	1000

Write these in Roman numerals.

Your age _____

12 _____

The number of people in your family _____

Your lucky number _____

The year _____

The number of legs on a chair _____

The number of faces on a cube _____

24 _____ 1672 _____

606 _____ 73 _____

58 _____ 99 _____

Name: _____

A closer look at clocks and watches

A closer look at sundials

Sundials (draw and write)

Name: _____

Measures in the past

Measuring using our bodies.

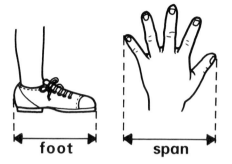

foot   span

stride   reach   arm   cubit

Big clocks

All about _____

(name of clock)

An idea web

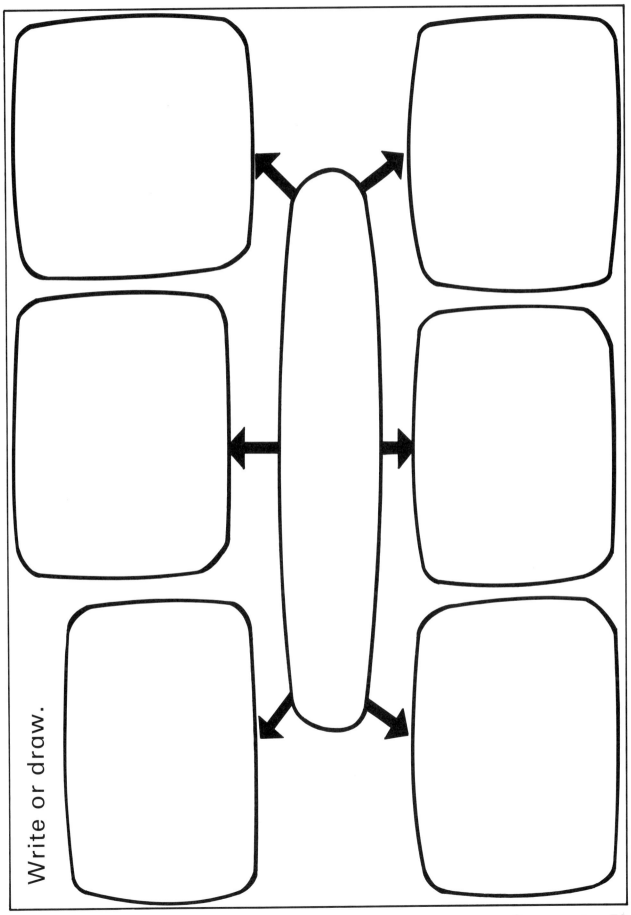

Write or draw.

Observation

I looked at _____

This is what I saw.
(write or draw)

Asking questions

Questions I want to ask.

Name: _____

A Victorian street scene

A Tudor street scene

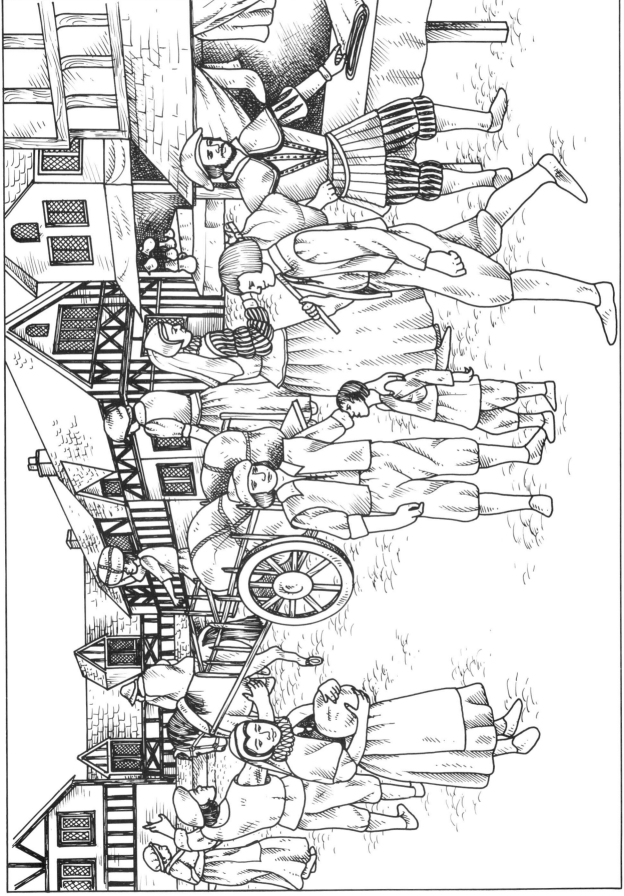

Library skills

A library quiz

How are the books sorted out in your school library?

_____

Story books are sometimes called 'fiction'. What are information books sometimes called?

_____

Find a history book in the library. What is its title?

_____

Keep a record of the history books from the school library that you think are useful.

Title	Why it is a useful book

Name: _____

Invaders in Britain

Medieval and Tudor times

Stuart times and Georgian rural life

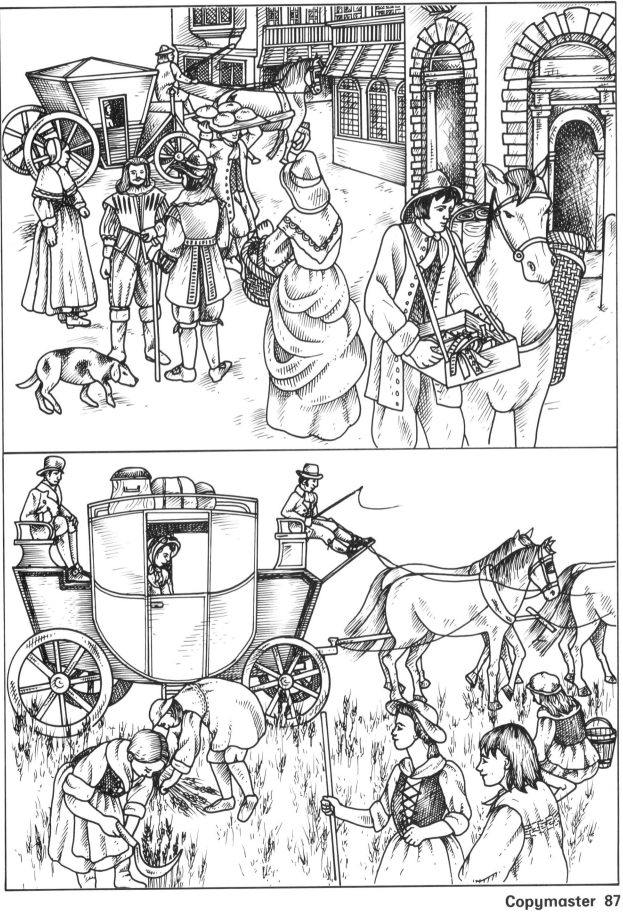

Name: _____

The Industrial Revolution

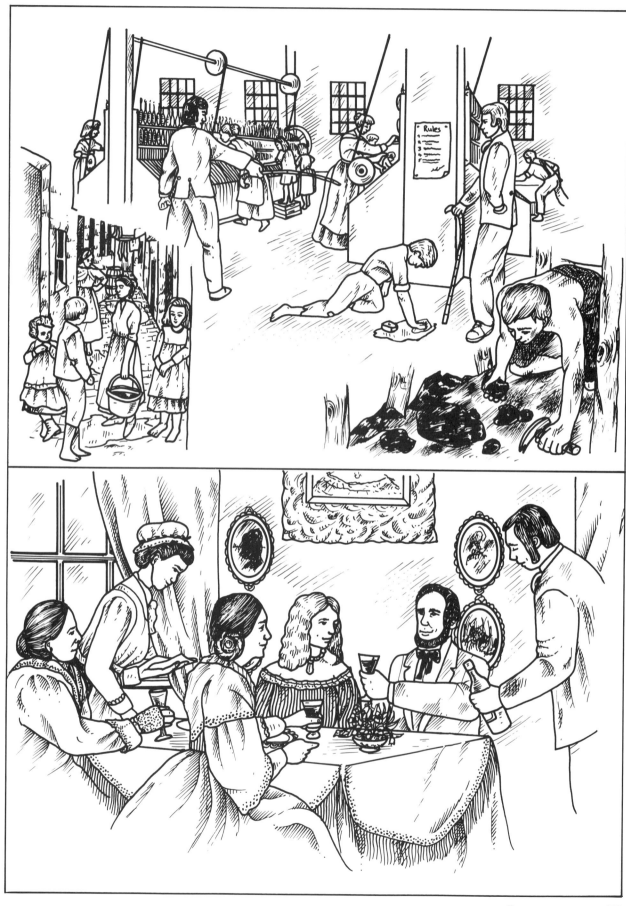

Victorian Britain

Into the twentieth century

After the Second World War

Selecting information

A grown-up I know well _____

_____

Write or draw the five most important things you will tell **your** grandchildren about this grown-up.

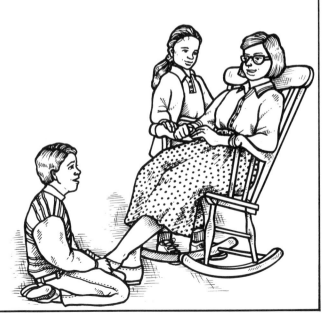

Name: _____

What's wrong?

What's wrong?

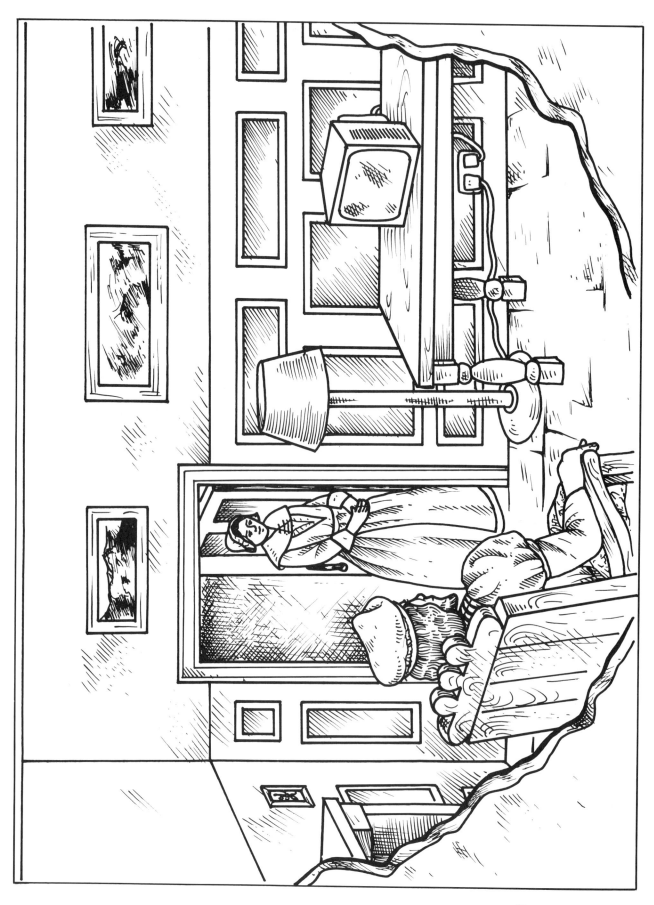

Name: _____

What's wrong?

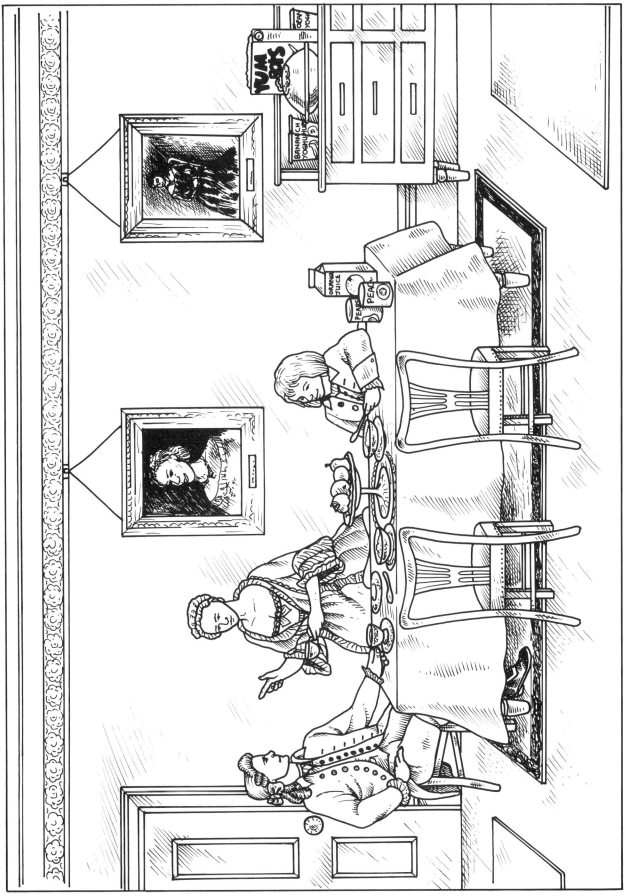

What's wrong?

Self-appraisal sheet

Name _____

When you can do a thing, tick the box.
Then take this sheet to your teacher.

		Teacher's initials
I can set myself a question to answer about the past.		
I can draw an idea web.		
I can observe well.		
I can give an opinion and listen to others.		
I can think of questions to ask about the past.		
I can write down questions to ask about the past.		
I can find clues about the past in pictures.		
I know what the parts of a book are.		
I can find a history book I want in the library.		
I can get information from a database.		
I can put information in a database.		
I can find important clues in pictures and say why I think they are important.		
I can find important clues in stories and say why I think they are important.		
I can talk about differences between two reports about the same thing.		
I can tell other people about my discoveries.		
I can draw things from the past to show what they looked like.		
I can write in a way that is best for what I want to say (diary, story, poem, report).		
I can do research on my own.		

Copymaster 97

Summary sheet

Name of child _____

Date _____	Date _____
Topic _____	Topic _____
Level and comments	*Level and comments*
AT 1	**AT 1**
AT 2	**AT 2**
AT 3	**AT 3**

Date _____	Date _____
Topic _____	Topic _____
Level and comments	*Level and comments*
AT 1	**AT 1**
AT 2	**AT 2**
AT 3	**AT 3**